Lip Sink and Francesca Clark Productions
in collaboration with Richard Jordan Productions present

MUSH AND ME
Karla Crome
from an idea conceived and developed by Daniella Isaacs and Rosy Banham

Mush and Me received its World Premiere as part of the 2014 Edinburgh Festival Fringe at the Underbelly. The production subsequently transferred to the Bush Theatre, London in November 2014, and then to JW3, London and Holden Street Theatres, Adelaide in February 2015. Post-Edinburgh the production was produced by Lip Sink and Francesca Clark Productions in collaboration with Richard Jordan Productions, and in Australia also with Holden Street Theatres.

Mush and Me

By Karla Crome

A Lip Sink and Francesca Clark production
in collaboration with Richard Jordan Productions

GABBY	Daniella Isaacs
MUSH (to 20 November 2014)	David Mumeni
MUSH (from 22nd November 2014)	Jaz Deol

Director	Rosy Banham
Designer	Carla Goodman
Lighting Designer	Chris Withers
Composer	David Ridley
Dramaturg	Joel MacCormack

Producer	Francesca Clark
Collaborative Producer	Richard Jordan Productions

Inspiration

Mush and Me was inspired by Nancy Yetzes the 102-year-old Great Aunt of Daniella. When Nancy was in her twenties she fell in love with a non-Jewish man who proposed to her. She declined because she was fearful of how her family and community would react. She has been single ever since. Nancy grew up in the East end of London and has witnessed a huge amount of change over her long life. She is currently learning how to use a computer, attends 'Keep Fit' classes and plays cards weekly.

The producers wish to thank:

Fiona & Michael Sherling, Fiorella Massey, HighTide Festival Theatre, Harriet Pennington Legh, Hayley Kaimakliotis, Holly Kendrick, IdeasTap, Jaime & Daniel Benton, Joanna & Richard Humphreys, Larry Lipman, Luke Barnes, Mirain Jones, Nancy Yetzes, Natalie Imbruglia, Nick Leslau, Old Vic New Voices, National Youth Theatre, Charlotte Ritchie, Paul Sonnabend, Rachel Tyson, Steven Atkinson, Miriam Margolyes, Stuart Peters, Vanessa Feltz and Sylvia Young.

CAST

Daniella Isaacs (Gabby)
Daniella trained at The Oxford School of Drama and is an alumni of the National Youth Theatre.
Theatre includes: *Long Story Short* (West Yorkshire Playhouse); *Defining Moments, Eye /Balls, Eating Ice Cream on Gaza Beach* (Soho Theatre); *Our Days of Rage* (The Old Vic Tunnels).
Film includes: *Fogbound, Maybe Older*.
Television includes: *Holby City, Skins, Night and Day, Burnside*.

David Mumeni (Mush to 20 November 2014)
David trained at Drama Centre.
Theatre includes: *The Machine* (Donmar Warehouse, Manchester International Festival & Park Avenue Armory, New York); *Tis Pity She's A Whore* (Cheek by Jowl, Barbican & International Tour); *Ten* (Royal Court).
Film includes: *Noble, The Inbetweeners Movie*.
Television includes: *PhoneShop, Cuckoo, Fresh Meat, Whitechapel, & Confessions from the Underground*.
David has recently finished filming *The Jesus Code* playing the role of Judas.

Jaz Deol (Mush from 22 November 2014)
Theatre includes: *The Djinns Of Eidgah* (Royal Court); *Harlesden High Street* (Tara Arts & Jackdaw Theatre); *Snookered* (Bush Theatre); *The Snow Queen* (Trestle Arts)
Film includes: *The Show, Honeycomb Lodge*
Television includes: *Code of a Killer*

COMPANY

Karla Crome
Writer

Karla is best known for her acting work. She played Riley in Sky Atlantic's *Hit and Miss* alongside US star Chloe Sevigny. She subsequently worked with globally acclaimed director of *The Killing*, Birger Larsen, in the BAFTA award winning *Murder* for BBC2, in which she played the lead, Coleen. Both performances won her a place in Screen International's 2012 *Stars of Tomorrow*, one of the most influential new talent roundups in the business (past candidates include Keira Knightley, Andrew Garfield and Dominic Cooper). Karla played series lead Jess in E4 flagship drama *Misfits* and most recently worked on Hit US drama *Under The Dome*.

Karla's writing work includes *Our Days of Rage*, (cowritten for the Old Vic Tunnels), which explored the devastation caused by the Arab Spring. NYT subsequently commissioned Karla to write *If Chloe Can*, a stage play about the pressures young women face when considering career options. The play has been developed and is currently touring UK universities.

Rosy Banham
Director

Directing includes: *England Street, If You're Glad I'll Be Frank* (Burton Taylor Studio, Oxford Playhouse); *One Under, Edges* (Edinburgh Fringe); *Charity Begins at Home* (Waterloo East). Assistant directing includes: *Things We Do For Love* (Theatre Royal Bath & UK Tour); *Bracken Moor* (Tricycle); *NSFW, The Witness* (Royal Court); *A Kind of Alaska, Krapp's Last Tape, Coasting* (all Bristol Old Vic); *Dick Whittington* (Oxford Playhouse); *The Comedy of Errors* (Tobacco Factory).

Carla Goodman
Designer

Carla Goodman is a set and costume designer working in theatre and opera. Her recent design credits include *Theatre Uncut* (Traverse, Soho Theatre and UK tour); *Listen, We're Family* (Wilton's Music Hall); *Ariodante* (Royal Academy of Music); *I am your Neighbour* (Oval House – site-specific); *King Lear* (Oval House Theatre); *Miss Nightingale* (New Wolsey Theatre and UK Tour); *A New Face for Fast Times* (Soho Theatre); *The Love Project* (Arts Depot and UK Tour); *NOLA* (Underbelly Edinburgh); *Heroes* (Only Connect); Royal Academy of Dance – Step Live! (Southbank Centre); *Kitchen to Measure* (Arcola Theatre); *Mr*

Happiness (Old Vic Tunnels); *Bud Take the Wheel* (Underbelly Edinburgh) and *Danny's Deal* (Old Vic New Voices tour). As assistant designer credits include: *The Drowned Man* (Punchdrunk); *Elephantom* (National Theatre Shed); *Nabucco* (De Vlaamse Opera Antwerp and Ghent); *Prince Igor* (Opernhaus Zurich and Staatsoper Hamburg); *Heart of Darkness* (Royal Opera House); *The Railway Children* (Eurostar Waterloo).

Chris Withers
Lighting Designer
Lighting Design credits include: *Jack and the Beanstalk, Puss in Boots, Robin Hood, Aladdin, Heavy Like the Weight of a Flame, The Temperamentals* (Greenwich Theatre); *Hamlet, Thebes, Reptember, The Talented Mr Ripley, Romeo and Juliet, Joan of Arc* (The Faction at New Diorama Theatre); *Lucy and the Hawk* (Northern Stage and Oval House); *What the Animals Say* (Hull Truck and Northern Stage); *Othello, Hedda Gabler* (UK and Ireland tour); *A Quiet Life, Blind Date/27 Wagons full of Cotton* (Riverside Studios*); Hindle Wakes, December Man, Saturn Returns and The Killing of Mr Toad* (Finborough Theatre); *Change* (Arcola), *The Great British Country Fete* (Bush Theatre and Tour); *Gutted- A Revenger's Musical* (Assembly Ballroom, Edinburgh); *Dirty White Boy - Tales of Soho* (Trafalgar Studios); *What's Wrong With Angry?* (King's Head); *The Canterbury Tales* (Battersea Arts Centre) Recent credits as an assistant/associate include: *The Seagull* (Southwark Playhouse); *Precious Little Talent* (Trafalgar Studios); *Lingua Franca* (59E59 New York*); Little Fish* (Finborough); *Well* (Apollo Shaftesbury Ave) and *How to Disappear Completely and Never be Found* (Southwark Playhouse).
www.chriswithers.co.uk
@xryz

David Ridley
Composer
David is an associate composer with Bucket Club and Tap Tap Theatre companies. He gained a Masters in Composition from the University of Bristol where he studied as a full Faculty of Arts Scholar, and spent 6 months in East China where he served as the inaugural conductor of The Voices of Hangzhou Youth Choir. Recent theatrical composition work includes *Lorraine and Alan* (Bucket Club) which won the 2014 MTN award for innovation in music theatre; *The Beasts* (Bucket Club, Lyric Hammersmith and tour); *Captain Morgan and the Sands of Time* (TapTap Theatre), and orchestration work: *Hansel and Gretel* (Royal Ballet); *The Secret of Crickley Hall* (Dan Jones, BBC1).

David also writes concert music and is in demand as a composer for choirs and chamber ensembles.

To listen to David's original music for *Mush and Me*, along with more of his work, please follow: www.davidjridley.co.uk.

Lip Sink
Producer
Lip Sink was founded in 2014 by performer and producer Daniella Isaacs, director Rosy Banham and writer Karla Crome. The company aims to create risk-taking new work influenced by real-life interviews with young adults. Their debut production, *Mush and Me*, received the Ideas Tap Underbelly Award and was performed at the Underbelly during the Edinburgh Fringe Festival in 2014. The production was subsequently shortlisted for the Brighton Fringe Award and announced as the Winner of the Holden Street Theatres Award.

Francesca Clark
Producer
Francesca is an independent theatre producer and project manager, as well as being Producer at HighTide Festival Theatre. Producing as part of HighTide Festival Theatre includes: *peddling* by Harry Melling (Off Broadway, Arcola, HighTide Festival); *Bottleneck* by Luke Barnes (Soho Theatre, UK tour, Pleasance & Underbelly Edinburgh); *Incognito* by Nick Payne (Bush Theatre, Live Theatre, Newcastle, North Wall, HighTide Festival); *The Big Meal* by Dan LeFranc (Theatre Royal Bath, HighTide Festival); *The Girls Guide to Saving the World* by Elinor Cook (HighTide Festival); *Stuart: A Life Backwards* by Alexander Masters adapted by Jack Thorne (Underbelly Edinburgh, Sheffield Theatres, Watford Palace Theatre); *Neighbors* by Branden Jacobs-Jenkins (Nuffield Theatre, HighTide Festival); *Smallholding* by Chris Dunkley (Soho Theatre, Nuffield Theatre, HighTide Festival); *Boys* by Ella Hickson (Soho Theatre, Nuffield Theatre , HighTide Festival); *Mudlarks* by Vickie Donoghue (Bush Theatre, 503, HighTide Festival); *Lidless* by Frances Ya-Chu Cowhig (Trafalgar Studios, Underbelly Edinburgh, HighTide Festival) *Stovepipe* by Adam Brace (Bush Theatre, National Theatre).

Awards: 2012 and 2010 Fringe First Awards for *Educating Ronnie* and *Lidless*; 2009 Whatsonstage Award nomination for Best Off-West End Production (*Stovepipe*).

www.francescaclark.com

Richard Jordan Productions

Collaborative Producer

Richard Jordan Productions is an Olivier and TONY Award-winning production company based in London under the artistic leadership of producer Richard Jordan. Founded in 1998, his company has produced over 190 productions in the UK as well as 19 other countries, including 60 world premieres and 70 European, Australian or US premieres enjoying associations with many of the world's leading theatres and arts organisations. Described by *The Stage* newspaper as 'one of the UK's most prolific theatre producers', Richard was the first recipient of the TIF/Society of London Theatre Producers Award and a finalist in the British Council Creative Entrepreneur Award. In 2009 for his work in the UK and international theatre industries he was selected for life time inclusion in A & C Black's annual publication *Who's Who*.

Richard has been at the forefront of developing and presenting works by a diverse range of established and emerging UK and international writers and artists such as: Alan Ayckbourn; Conor McPherson; Omphile Molusi; Alan Bennett; Cora Bissett; Athol Fugard; David Greig; Martin McDonagh; Valentijn Dhaenens; Cristian Ceresoli; Christopher Durang; Nick Steur; Pieter de Buysser; Robert Farquhar; the Q Brothers; Heather Raffo; Stefan Golaszewski and Belgian collective Ontroerend Goed whose work he co-produces worldwide. His productions have won a number of awards including: the TONY Award for Best Play; the Olivier Award for Outstanding Achievement at an Affiliate Theatre; the Emmy Award for Best Feature section; eight Scotsman Fringe Firsts Awards; two Herald Angel Awards; six Total Theatre Awards; The Spirit of the Fringe Award; the Off-West End Award; three Helen Hayes Awards; the Adelaide Festival Award; the US Black Alliance Award; Stage Award; Obie Award; the John Gassner Award for Best New American Play; Jeff Award; the Lucille Lortel Award; and the Drama Desk; Drama League; New York Critics, ; Outer Critic Circle Best New Play Awards.

Richard has enjoyed a long association with the Bush Theatre where between 2006 and 2012 he served as an Associate Artist. His past productions at the Bush Theatre include; *Nine Parts of Desire*, which he subsequently also produced in New York and across North America, *Monsieur Ibrahim and the Flowers of the Qur'an, Chapel Street,* which both also toured nationally and *The Stefan Golaszewski Plays.*

Holden Street Theatres, Adelaide
(Australian season Co-Producer)

Holden Street Theatres is a venue and production house located in South Australia that began in 2002. Holden Street Theatres presents productions from all over the world and tours work locally and in the UK.

With a strong focus on creative and artistic merit, Holden Street Theatres prides itself on presenting work that will enhance the local industry and cultural life.

In 2008 Holden Street Theatres created the Holden Street Theatres' Edinburgh Award, presented annually at the Edinburgh Fringe. The award winning production is then produced with Holden Street Theatres the following year at the Adelaide Fringe. Many of these productions have subsequently gone on to win awards for Best Theatre in production and performance every year since the awards creation at the Adelaide Fringe Awards in both peer and media-judged award ceremonies.

Mush and Me is the recipient of the 2014 Holden Street Theatres Adelaide Fringe Award.

Other awards Holden Street Theatres has received includes, Best Overall Production at the Adelaide Fringe, Best Venue, Best Puppetry, Best Performer, Best Theatre and Good Partnering Recognition from the Australian Business Arts Foundation.

About JW3

The aim of JW3 is to transform the Jewish landscape in London by helping to create a vibrant, diverse and proud community, inspired by and engaged in Jewish arts, culture and community.

The size of our ambition is reflected both in the scale and elegance of our new building and in the creativity and energy of our programme. The role of JW3 is to offer outstanding events, activities, classes and courses that increase the quality, variety and volume of Jewish conversation in London and beyond, reflecting the diversity of our community.

BUSH THEATRE

We make theatre for London. Now.

The Bush is a **world-famous** home for new plays and an internationally renowned champion of plays. We **discover, nurture and produce** the best new playwrights from the widest range of backgrounds from our home in a distinctive corner of west London.

The Bush has won over **100 awards** and developed an enviable reputation for touring its acclaimed productions nationally and internationally.

We are excited by exceptional new voices, stories and perspectives – particularly those with **contemporary bite** which reflect the **vibrancy of British culture** now.

Now located in a recently renovated library building on the Uxbridge Road in the heart of Shepherd's Bush, the theatre houses a 144-seat auditorium, rehearsal rooms and a lively café bar.

bushtheatre.co.uk

'A powerhouse of new writing'

Sunday Times Culture

Karla Crome

MUSH AND ME

OBERON BOOKS
LONDON

WWW.OBERONBOOKS.COM

First published in 2014 by Oberon Books Ltd

521 Caledonian Road, London N7 9RH

Tel: +44 (0) 20 7607 3637 / Fax: +44 (0) 20 7607 3629

e-mail: info@oberonbooks.com

www.oberonbooks.com

A catalogue record for this book is available from the British
Library.

PB ISBN: 978-1-78319-206-9

E ISBN: 978-1-78319-705-7

Cover image: Chloe Wicks/Francesca Tortora

Printed, bound and converted
by CPI Group (UK) Ltd, Croydon, CR0 4YY.

Visit www.oberonbooks.com to read more about all our books
and to buy them. You will also find features, author interviews and
news of any author events, and you can sign up for e-newsletters
so that you're always first to hear about our new releases.

SCENE 1

1.30 pm, Monday 9 June. The 'Central Office Solutions' North London Branch. MUSHTAQ 'MUSH' NOURREDINE is sitting at a desk, his legs on the table, computer in front of him. He sits opposite an empty desk space, more 'lived in' but tidy nonetheless. MUSH wears the office standard cordless headset, he is schmoozing a client. **BOLD TYPE indicates the character is on the phone.**

MUSH: **...That's basically inclusive of anything that runs off a plug socket. So we cover landline telephones, routers, overhead projectors, iPads...you use iPads, yeah?**

Laptops then?

No, no not at all, listen –

He checks the screen.

– Heidi –

What kind of name is *that*?

between you and me, Heidi, you've dodged a bullet. They're a con. You know they design all their products to break in two years?

So you'll go out and buy another one!

You can get a tablet from Tesco for half the price that does exactly the same thing.

Yeah, but when it comes to that stuff I'm impartial, you know what I mean? So you can trust me.

No problem.

So you interested?

GABRIELLA 'GAB' KEHLMANN enters. 24, smartly dressed. She looks on edge. Her hands are shaking. She stops dead at the sight of MUSH. MUSH looks at her –

GAB: Hi, what's this/ about?

MUSH silences her with his hand.

MUSH: **Say it again, Heidi, sorry?**

GAB's embarrassed, she sits down at her desk. Logs in, puts on her headset. As MUSH continues his conversation, GAB logs into her own computer.

Yeah? Great.

Beat. He looks at GAB, checks her out a bit. She looks at him. He looks away.

Absolutely. What I'm gonna do is forward you a quote via email and put my name and number at the top. Then you can get in touch if you've got any questions at all.

Even about iPads.

Thats right, hahaha.

I also do...uh...marriage counselling and palm reading.

MUSH glances at GAB.

Alright then. Thanks Heidi. Take care now. Bye.
Whats up?

GAB: Where's Louise?

MUSH: What?

GAB: That's Louise's desk. Wheres Louise?

MUSH: I dunno, babe. I got moved here.

GAB: From where?

MUSH: **Hello, am I speaking to Mrs Sutherland?/**

He points upwards.

GAB: Why?

MUSH gestures – hold on –

Good Afternoon Madam, how are you? I'm calling from Central Office Solutions. We specialise in providing insurance for *(She hangs up.)* Suck me off then. *(To GAB.)* Check your emails.

GAB: Excuse me?

MUSH: Head office implemented a branch shake-up.

GAB: When?

MUSH: Check your inbox, there's a memo.

GAB checks her emails, whilst pulling on her headset.

GAB: 'Competitive Sales Strategy'.

MUSH: Yeah like, performance motivation.

GAB: I can see that.

MUSH: Weren't my idea.

GAB: So, because you and I dominate the leaderboard they want us to – what exactly? Wrestle it out? **Hello, am I speaking to Mr Holden?**

MUSH: It's a bit of musical chairs. Don't stress about it.

Mr Holden, hi. Gabriella Kehlmann here, calling from Central Office Solutions. How are you getting on? Good. Mr Holden, we've recently updated our insurance package and as a former customer we can offer systems protection at a heavily reduced rate. *(Covering the mouthpiece.)* I'm not stressed, it just doesn't make any sense to do that with *high* achievers, does it? Do it with probationaries.

MUSH: They probably do.

GAB: Oh, I'm sorry to hear that.

GAB: **I see. Listen, I'm not entirely qualified to help you with that, this is the sales department, but I'm going**

to pass you on to someone in customer services, alright?

Just hold for a second.

GAB presses the mute button on her headset.

MUSH: There isn't a customer service, babe.

GAB: I'm aware of that. Did you get this rota as well? I don't work Friday afternoons. They know that.

MUSH shrugs.

GAB: Right. Sorry – I'm going to complain about this.

MUSH: Relax.

GAB: I'm fine.

MUSH: Your hands are shaking.

GAB: That's a Benign Essential Tremor.

Beat.

From caffeine.

MUSH: Ok.

Beat. She begins to type. GAB doesn't look up as they talk.

MUSH: How many units do you shift a week, then?

GAB: New or repeats?

MUSH: Both.

GAB: I don't know. Depends. Erm…15?

MUSH: Is that it?

Beat. GAB points at her laptop screen.

GAB: We're 'joint' leaders. You must be averaging out the same.

MUSH: It's a slow quarter.

GAB: I wouldn't know – I've only been here 3 weeks.

MUSH: Three *weeks*?

GAB: And apparently I'm already top regional sales. So from what I can tell, a spastic could do this job.

MUSH: Actually, it can get –

GAB silences MUSH with her finger. She now speaks to Mr. Holden in a Regional Accent different from her own. As she talks, she takes a tub of hummus and half a packet of Ryvitas out of her handbag.

GAB: **Hello, Mr Holden? This in Angela from Customer Service – so sorry to hear about the miscommunication with the February order. Can you tell me a little more?**

Uh huh. Yeah.

Right, right.

That *is* totally unacceptable.

Look, here's what I'll do. I'm gonna talk to Gabby in sales and I will try my very best to get you the new software update at 20% off. Ok?

Not at all. No guarantees though, Mr Holden. Alright? Bu-bye!

GAB taps the mute button.

MUSH: Is that hummus?

GAB: Yes.

MUSH: Did you make it?

GAB: My dad did. Why?

MUSH: Your dad cooks?

GAB: So?

MUSH: Nuffin. A packed lunch, innit. Cute.

GAB glares.

MUSH: It's nice. I wish someone would do that for me.

GAB: It's a tub of left over dip.

MUSH: I'm saying it looks good. Tasty.

GAB: **Hello Mr Holden?**

Over her dialogue, GAB spreads the hummus over the Ryvitas. MUSH watches her.

Right, I'm being told I'm to give you 20 percent off your software excess? Is that what you were told? Ok then – that's fine, but I have to ask that you pay today as I think heads will roll if my boss gets wind! / Ok then? That's 306 pounds and 48 pence, is it a Visa as before?

GAB lifts a Ryvita to her mouth, but clocks MUSH watching. She lowers the food.

Can you confirm the last three digits on the back of the card? Great. That's all gone through, and i'm so sorry about all this stress!

Not at all.

Have a great day. Bye.

MUSH: That's not a 20 percent discount.

GAB: He doesn't know that. He was about 300 years old.

MUSH laughs.

MUSH: You know they record the calls?

GAB: So? As long as you're making money, they don't care what you do. You and I are too valuable.

MUSH: You're an actor, innit.

GAB: No.

MUSH: Yes you are.

GAB: No, I'm – **Hello, can I speak to Mr. Odewayo please?**

MUSH: Loads of actors work here.

GAB: I'm a lawyer.

MUSH snorts.

In training.

MUSH: What you doing here, then?

GAB: It's a brief stopgap.

MUSH: Oh, it's a 'brief stopgap.'

MUSH's headset beeps.

GAB: I've just come from an interview with a Law Firm.

MUSH: Oh yeah?

GAB: Yeah.

MUSH: **Hello, Mushtaq speaking.** Did you get it?

Beat. GAB shifts awkwardly.

Ohhh shit, what you do? **Hello?**

MUSH frowns slightly. Lowers his voice.

I told you to call me on my mobile. You can't use this line. I'm fine. Yes. Yes Mum. Yeah – Bye.

Beat.

GAB: Does your mum call you every day?

MUSH: What's it to you?

GAB: Nothing. *'Cute'.* **Mr Odewayo? This is Gabriella calling from Central Office Solutions. We specialise in providing insurance for Small Businesses, and as a newly registered company I wanted to just familiarise you with our latest equipment protection plan. Is that**

something you'd be interested in? *(Covering mic.)* Can you do me a favour?

MUSH: Me?

GAB nods.

GAB: **And can i ask how much you're currently paying?** Would you mind covering me on Friday? **Ok – can you bear with me while I...uh...liaise with Accounts? Thank you.**

She mutes the headset.

Please? I don't work Fridays. If you just cover me this week I can sort something long-term.

MUSH: Actually – I can't, you know. Sorry.

GAB: Why?

MUSH: Gotta see a man about a dog.

Beat.

GAB: Can you reschedule?

MUSH: Can you?

GAB: I'll cover any of your independent shifts this week.

MUSH: Sorry.

GAB: Louise always covered me on a Friday.

MUSH: Louise is a mug.

GAB: It's really important.

MUSH: Not being funny, but I don't even know you. I'm not gonna come in 'cause you and your mates wanna get fingered in fucking...Mahikis.

GAB: I beg your pardon?

MUSH: The rota isn't fixed around your social life, babe.

GAB: I'm not asking you because i want to go *out*.

MUSH: So work then.

GAB: Its an important *family* event, that i absolutely cannot miss.

MUSH: What, every single week?

GAB: Do this one thing for me, just this week, and that'll be it. I promise I won't ask you to/ do anything –

He points at the hummus.

MUSH: Gimme that.

Beat.

GAB: No.

MUSH: I'll do your shift for the hummus.

GAB: I haven't eaten all day.

MUSH: You look like you haven't eaten all month.

GAB: Fuck you.

MUSH: I'm saying you're thin! It's a compliment.

GAB: I'll bring you some tomorrow?

GAB: You're incredibly immature.

MUSH: You're incredibly immature.

Beat.

GAB: Whatever. Take it.

MUSH take off his headset and heads to GAB's desk. GABBY moves back her chair a fraction. MUSH gathers GAB's entire lunch.

GAB: Can I at least have half?

MUSH: I dunno, you know. I'm pretty hungry.

MUSH takes his winnings back to his desk.

GAB: SHIT. **Hello, Mr Odewayo, are you still there?**

MUSH puts his headset back on.

Thanks for waiting! Accounts have agreed not just to match that price but to lower it by…erm…10 pounds. How does that sound?

I don't want you to miss out Mr Odewayo the offer is only going to stand for today… No? Ok. I totally understand. Ok.

Bye. Have they blocked Facebook from the Server?

MUSH: You need to download a separate IP address, so it's off the network.

GAB sighs.

MUSH: Gimme your email. I'll send you a link.

Beat.

Babe. If I wanted to try it I wouldn't inbox you an IP address. **Hello, can I speak to…uh…Rima Chedidi? Hi! Ha, you've got the same name as my Grandma Rima. I'm calling from – I said, you've got the same name as my grandmother…I said YOU SHARE MY GRANDMOTHER'S NAME.**

*Where the bold type appears in **italics** MUSH speaks Lebanese Arabic.*

Is this Chedidi Glassware? Rima – *Where are you from? Yes! I do, I thought you might be Lebanese! Listen, I'm calling from Central Office Solutions, we are a small business insurance provider, do you have insurance for any of your office equipment?*

GAB looks at MUSH with a little of the same wonder he showed her earlier.

Sure, he can call me back at anytime. My name is Mushtaq, ok? Great. Thank you, dear. Bye!

GAB: Did you know her?

MUSH: Nope.

GAB: Right.

Beat.

MUSH: You know, hummus messed my car up once.

GAB: You what?

MUSH: Completely fucked my exhaust.

GAB: Hummus fucked your exhaust.

MUSH: I know, it's so stupid. It was my cousin's wedding, and where I'm from, you know, it's all about the food at weddings. So I was picking up my mum from Asda and she had loads of shopping bags, maybe 20. Like a stupid amount. Anyways, she obviously forgot about one. So, I was backing up and I went straight over a whole load of it. Hummus, I mean.

GAB: And it went in the engine? How?

MUSH: Must've exploded up over the tyres. Then I got proper vexed cos I went over some of that Taramasalata too.

GAB looks a little confused.

Yeah. There was a sign next to the – uh – you know – the parking space. It said 'Caution – dips in the road.'

GAB smiles.

GAB: That is truly atrocious.

MUSH: Ooooooh is that a smile?

GAB: You've been googling hummus jokes for 10 minutes.

MUSH: No.

GAB: Sad.

MUSH: I just had to check you weren't a robot. 'Cos I can't compete with a robot.

GAB shakes her head. Grins.

MUSH: Wow. That's a pretty smile.

GAB: I still need cover on Friday.

MUSH: Yeah.

GAB: Will you do it, then?

MUSH: I said I would. I'm a man of my word.

GAB: Really?

MUSH: Yes! I got you.

GAB: Ok.

Beat.

It's Gabby, in case you –

MUSH: **Hello, Can I talk to Paris Hayward please?** What's up Gab. Mush.

SCENE 2

In The Metropolitan Bar (Baker Street Wetherspoons) **8 pm Friday 13 June.** *MUSH and GAB sit opposite each other. A couple of empty wine glasses next to GAB. Maybe a shot glass. MUSH sips on a J20. The centrepiece is a Bacon Burger.*

MUSH: No.

GAB: Ah…come on.

MUSH: No.

GAB: Why?

MUSH: 'Cos I don't *want* to. It reeks.

GAB: I'm going to.

MUSH: Go on then.

She pulls two rashers of bacon out of the burger with her fingertips. She hesitates.

MUSH: See? You're full of it. Send it back, man.

GAB: I can eat around it.

MUSH: You could sue.

GAB: Aren't you even a tiny bit curious?

MUSH: Pigs eat their own shit, you know.

Beat.

GAB: They don't.

MUSH: They do! I watched this documentary once about some tribe in the mountains in Africa or somewhere like that. Guess what they did? This is *so* nasty, right – this tribe, yeah, the human beings, I mean – they had this sewage system where they shat on this slide, and the shit went straight down to the pigs' troughs. And the pigs ate it.

GAB: Did the humans eat the pigs?

MUSH: Why else would you keep them?

GAB: Disgusting.

MUSH: Have you read *Animal Farm*?

GAB: Yes.

MUSH: Basically these pigs take over this farm and –

GAB: I know what it's about, yeah –

MUSH: Yeah, so at the end the most evil pig walks around on his hind legs like a human. I remember reading it at school and that just made me hate them even more.

Imagine a pig walking towards you on its back legs, yeah, with a little jacket on. That would scare me so much.

GAB: They have incredibly intense orgasms.

Beat.

MUSH: Pigs?

GAB: They orgasm for up to 30 minutes. And when they ejaculate there's like, a litre of sperm.

Beat.

MUSH: Ha…

GAB: No, they do. It's a fact. Look it up if you want.

MUSH makes a face.

MUSH: A litre of jizz.

GAB: Yep. Imagine that.

MUSH: I don't have to.

GAB raises an eyebrow. Touché.

GAB: You're funny. Have some wine.

MUSH: I don't really drink. I just came with Erik.

GAB: It's Friday!

MUSH: Yeah – Didn't you have something to do today?

GAB: It looks like skin doesn't it?

MUSH: The bacon?

GAB: Mmmm.

MUSH: And you wanna eat it?

GAB: Why shouldn't I? Everyone else does.

She brings it to her mouth – hesitates.

MUSH: What's stopping you?

GAB: I don't know. Habit?

MUSH: Do you wanna get some proper food, then? Have you been to Maroush yet? On Edgware Road?

GAB: I just wanna get fucked, to be honest.

MUSH: Do you actually *like* it here?

GAB: Don't you?

MUSH: Wetherspoons? Are you high?

GAB: What? Good for picking up girls, isn't it?

MUSH: Yeah, but I'm not fucking… Phil Mitchell. I do have a bit of taste.

GAB: You're on Tinder.

MUSH: So?

GAB: You're not going to find love on a dating app.

MUSH: It's not 'love' that I'm after, though, is it?

GAB: Hang on. You won't eat bacon, but you're happy to have sex with a stranger every weekend?

Beat.

I mean, I'm *assuming* sex before marriage is a sin in Islam? Or…?

MUSH: It's different, man.

GAB: How?

MUSH shakes his head.

How? I really want to know. Honestly.

MUSH: Eating bacon – that's like – that's like a *choice*. A man can go without bacon. He can't go without sex. Blue balls. It hurts.

Beat.

Sorry.

GAB: No! No. I *agree*. If your casual sex isn't hurting anyone, then what's the problem?

GABBY's phone rings. She turns it off. Throws it in her bag.

MUSH: I guess you have to go soon.

GABBY: I don't *have* to do anything.

MUSH: You said you have that family thing on Fridays. I thought it was a big deal or something?

GAB: What, shabbat? Haha! *(Taking the piss.)* Oy vey! Ve cannot miss the shabbas dinner! Do you know, right, according to *my* esteemed faith, on Friday night, you're not allowed to switch on the bathroom light to take a piss? I mean, I get refraining from murder and rape and stealing…but some things are just fucking *ridiculous*. You for instance – why can't you share a glass of wine with me?

MUSH: Feisty aren't you?

GAB: Have some wine.

MUSH: It's Haram.

GAB: And yet you'll still have pre-marital sex. So have some wine.

MUSH: No.

GAB: *Why?*

MUSH: It makes people act stupid.

GAB: And does bacon make you act stupid? I mean, is it ethically worse to eat a pig, than – say – a cow?

Hmm?

EXACTLY. It's stupid. Some people don't have a choice what to eat.

MUSH: Like who?

GAB: The little starving Africans and that.

MUSH: Passing on a sausage is not going to cure world hunger.

GAB picks up MUSH's J20.

GAB: Do you like these?

MUSH: Erm…

Not really allowing time for a response, she downs a few gulps of the J20 then chucks a shot in the bottle. Over her dialogue she shakes up her new concoction and she finishes her wine.

GAB: I can't think of one major world religion that encourages any sort of fucking…*indulgence.* It's all abstinence. What's wrong with *indulging*?

'Oh – no thanks, no, I'm alright, I'll just sit here with a plastic bag on my head, pissing in the dark.'

She has a few sips of her Vodka/J20. Pauses for a second.

Do you remember Reefs? The drink, Reef?

Beat.

What I'm saying is, in what universe is it sinful to eat a burger?!

Well. Piss on that. We're not harming anyone. We're having a private meal, eating what's already dead. If that offends my god or your god then what kind of vain, nosey megalomaniac is he?

MUSH: What?

GAB: I'm saying God's a control freak.

MUSH: If you created the entire world, you *would* be a control freak.

GAB: No. That's where you're wrong. If I created the world, I would face up to my responsibilities.

Beat.

This world is fucked, Mush. Seriously. It's undeniably fucked. And yet –

MUSH: It's *not* –

GAB: And YET – If you abuse your kids, you get locked up in prison. If you steal, cheat and lie, you get punished. But when God gives us tsunamis, genocides and gang-rape, we're all like: 'Cheers! Spank me harder!'.

So unless God is retarded, I don't believe it.

MUSH: Don't believe what?

GAB: In God. There is no God.

MUSH: Well I think there is.

GAB: Can you prove it?

MUSH: No. I just know there is.

GAB: *(Dripping with sarcasm.)* You must be *supremely blessed.* Congratulations. L'chaim!

GAB suddenly stuffs a rasher of bacon into her mouth, forcing it in with her fingers. It's very quick. She doesn't take her eyes off him, despite the unfamiliarity of the act and the taste. She's struggling with it a bit.

MUSH: Maaaaate.

She continues to chew. Stops for a beat. Seems as if she might wretch. Carries on. Swallows.

MUSH: Well?!

GAB: Mm.

MUSH: Is it nice?

GAB: I don't know. It's kind of salty.

MUSH: Can't believe you did that.

GAB starts to get a bit upset.

GAB: Chewy.

She realises the magnitude of what she's done and feels very guilty.

Fuck.

She puts away a few hefty gulps of wine. MUSH feels terrible.

MUSH: It's like you said though. If you don't believe in God… It don't matter.

GAB: My Dad's gonna kill me.

MUSH: You don't have to tell him.

GAB: I'm late.

MUSH: Do you want me to drop you home?

GAB: You can't.

MUSH: Why?

GAB: Oh yeah! Riding shotgun round Hampstead with an ARAB. Mother will be tickled pink.

MUSH: Yep, fair enough.

GAB: Not being rude, but…

MUSH: I get it. It's not my first rodeo.

GAB: They're not really fans of –

MUSH: Yeah. Mine too.

Beat.

Listen, I'm gonna bounce.

GAB snorts.

GAB: You're gonna *'bounce'*? Ok.

MUSH: I like you Gab, but you're being a bit of a dick. Bye.

MUSH moves to leave. GAB intercepts him.

GAB: Ah come on – don't go…

MUSH: I ain't gonna sit here getting mugged off –

GAB: Just, wait. Please.

MUSH: You're drunk.

GAB: Please? Please – PLEASE!

Beat. MUSH leads GAB back to the table.

MUSH: Gab?

GAB: Dad picked me up yesterday and I went to get some chewing gum out of the glove compartment of his car. There was a letter. From the hospital.

Beat.

He's got breast cancer.

MUSH lets out an involuntary laugh.

MUSH: Sorry. I didn't think… Can men even – ?

GAB: Well obviously they can.

MUSH: Not as bad as women though, surely? Does he actually have – uh –

GAB: It's spread. To his brain. Brain metastasis.

MUSH: Did you ask him about it?

GAB: No.

MUSH: Why not?

She looks at the food.

MUSH: That's tough, man. That's really tough. Is that why you're acting a bit…nuts. Like.

GAB: I'm scared.

MUSH: Aw…babe, come here.

He offers her a hug.

GAB: I don't need to cry into you, thanks. I'm not 3.

MUSH: Ok.

A beat. MUSH picks up the burger and takes a huge bite. He also struggles with it.

GAB: You didn't need to do that.

MUSH: No worse than eating a kebab, right?

GAB: Right.

Beat.

MUSH: Gabby – There is scientific proof for the existence of God.

GAB gives him a look.

There is. It's a theory about light particles. So a particle, or a particle of light, is called a photon. And a photon is basically something that can exist in one place and at every place at the same time. That's a scientific fact. And you know how God is seen as like, light? He can exist in one place and every place at the same time. It's a scientific way of looking at it. A particle of energy. What they call some functioning light I call Allah.

GAB: Allah.

MUSH: Allah, God – whatever.

GAB: Where did you learn that?

MUSH: I read it.

GAB: That's a clever theory but it doesn't *prove* anything.

MUSH: Doesn't *disprove*.

Beat. They stare at each other. GABBY leans in for a kiss. MUSH immediately pulls away.

MUSH: Woah.

GAB lets out a dry laugh.

MUSH: Listen. I think you're really attractive –

GAB: BUT I'm a Jew.

MUSH: What?! It's not even –

GAB: This is ridiculous.

MUSH: Babe.

GAB: Wow. I think I just got rejected by Ghetto Muslim, and now he's giving me bereavement counselling on Shabbat! This is priceless.

MUSH: You're right. I'm not the person you should be having this conversation with. Go home.

GAB: I think it's obvious that that's the last place I want to be, 'Mushtaq'.

Beat.

Sorry.

MUSH: From what you said these Friday evenings are really important to you and your dad. Get a coffee, sober up, go home.

Silence.

GAB: What time is it?

MUSH checks his watch.

MUSH: It's still pretty early. 8.30.

GAB: I'm already late.

MUSH: I can drop you near your house. Few streets away or something.

Beat.

If anyone asks you can say I'm a taxi driver.

Beat.

GAB smiles.

GAB: So. What's Allah's punishment for eating pork?

MUSH: He turns us into Jews.

SCENE 3

Monday 21 July. 8 pm. Southend-on-Sea. *GAB and MUSH sit on a bench at the pier. MUSH takes a bottle of champagne out of his backpack.*

GAB: What's this?

MUSH: That's booze…wait…close your eyes.

GAB: I don't like surprises.

MUSH pulls out GAB's tupperware box from Scene One, and a sandwich bag with 4 falafels. He arranges them on the bench.

MUSH: Ok.

GABBY opens her eyes.

GAB: Please don't tell me that's the same hummus I gave you, you absolute grotbag.

MUSH: Fuck off! It's Tahini!

GAB: I thought you weren't eating?

MUSH checks his watch.

MUSH: I can in a bit.

GABBY picks up the falafels.

GAB: Did you make these?

MUSH: Yeah. Try them.

GAB: I feel a bit rude.

MUSH: Have the champagne then.

GAB: Not now.

MUSH: Why not?! It's a celebration! Any other white girl would be sucking that off by now.

GAB: Have you got a cup?

MUSH: Ah PISS.

GAB rolls her eyes.

MUSH: Drink it from the bottle.

GAB: What – neck it down like a 13 year old?

MUSH: Who cares what you neck it from, it all ends up in the same place.

GAB shrugs – pops the cork.

MUSH: Wheeeeey! Mazeltov!

GAB giggles.

GAB: Idiot.

She takes a sip.

MUSH: Nice?

GAB: Very nice.

Beat.

GAB: Can you not watch me drink please?

MUSH looks away.

MUSH: I'm not looking.

GAB: If anyone asks we went to Brighton, ok? Frinton, even. NOT Southend.

MUSH: Do your parents know you're here?

GAB: No.

MUSH: I mean do they know who you're *with?*

GAB: Do yours?

Pause.

They think I'm at an induction day. It had to be a good excuse to leave my dad.

MUSH: Right. How is he?

GAB smiles.

GAB: He's good. You wouldn't even know he was… He's very vocal, anyway; Rowing with us about everything. Literally everything. The catering, the eulogy, the *casket.* He wanted a cheap one but Mum bought solid walnut, and he was like 'Fuck sakes Deb, what difference does it make? It's not like I'm gonna *know!*'.

She laughs. MUSH doesn't.

I thought it was quite funny, considering.

Pause.

MUSH: Look, I appreciate you bunking with me.

GAB: Well, I appreciate the invite. Thank you. This is very kind.

MUSH: No worries. Had to repay you for those sex dice, didn't I?

GAB: That was a *Dreidel.*

MUSH: Course it was.

GAB: I thought you'd find it interesting.

MUSH: I do! I really do. I'm gonna miss working with you.

Beat.

GAB: This is really so sweet   MUSH: I didn't think you'd –
of you –

39

GAB/MUSH: Sorry/Go on.

GAB: Go on.

MUSH: No, I was just gonna say, I was surprised you got the training contract.

GAB: Oh, thanks!

MUSH: No, I mean you were a bit shifty after the interview.

GAB: That's because it was a fucking disaster!

MUSH: Why?

GAB: The partner's an old family friend. He also happens to be my ex-boyfriend's uncle. He kept asking why we'd broken up and –

MUSH: I didn't know you had a boyfriend.

GAB: I don't. That's the whole point. 'Ex'. I kept trying to change the subject but he wouldn't let it go. Told him to piss off in the end.

MUSH: Must've been serious for him to ask –

GAB: Maybe right at the beginning we were – but…look. It was a hangover from Uni. He was so patronising. He thought my ambitions were *cute*. Anyway, he's got a willing little idiot to kiss his arse now. I wish them well.

MUSH: Yeaaaah, girl! You know this!

GAB: See, I can say that to you! I can't say it in interview at Lehmann and Chapman. Jews are so fucking incestuous. Everyone is someones cousin or sister or fiancé.

GAB opens the falafels and nibbles on one.

MUSH: I don't think that's just Jews, babe. That's Arabs, Greeks, Africans…

GAB: Oh, shit the bed!

MUSH: What?

GAB: I've started eating!

MUSH: Oh yeah, it's fine.

GAB: I'm being rude.

MUSH: It's my problem, not yours. Knock yourself out.

GAB pauses.

Honestly, I don't care.

GAB stays still.

Don't you like it?

GAB: You're really serious about this stuff.

MUSH: What, Ramadan?

GAB: Not just Ramadan, the whole Muslim *'thing'*.

MUSH: It's not a pair of fucking trainers.

GAB: But you're a rude boy.

MUSH: A rude boy?

GAB: I mean, you're very dedicated to it.

MUSH: Nowadays, yeah. I used to be a right little shit.

GAB: How so?

MUSH: Well, you know my cousin, Farouk?

GAB: I don't, but /yeah

MUSH: We used to roll – uh – hang around together, yeah? He's great but he's a bit dumb. Anyways he somehow got into dealing. Long story short he got raided and he went down for a bit.

GAB: For drug dealing.

MUSH: It was *weed*.

GAB: And you were helping him?

MUSH: Oi calm down man! It was like 3 baggys a week! Pocket money!

GAB: Right.

MUSH: Sorry, are you the police now or something?

GAB: I don't think it's funny.

MUSH: Neither do I. It was horrible, actually. My mum went nuts. She's always been a bit fucking *(He taps his head.)* – and she just flipped. Sent me to my uncle's in Lebanon. I started going Mosque with him. The Mosque! I haven't been there in years. Got me thinking…

GAB: About what?

Beat.

MUSH: I dunno…self-respect and that. I know you think it's all bollocks, but Allah's got a bigger plan for me than being some dickhead's weed man.

GAB: Then why are you working at a call centre?

MUSH: Easy –

GAB: I think you're more intelligent then that.

MUSH: You think being successful is better than being nice?

GAB: In my house it is.

Beat.

I'm *joking.*

MUSH: Still.

GAB: I'll fast with you tomorrow if you like.

Beat.

MUSH: Yeah? And what do I get out of that?

Beat. They smile.

MUSH: Do you know when Mohammed, peace be upon him, started Islam –

GAB: Yes, peace be upon him.

MUSH pushes her.

MUSH: Don't take the piss out of my prophet, you slag.

GAB: Is this going to be a real story or one of your atrocious jokes?

MUSH: When Mohammed –

GAB: Peace be upon him.

MUSH: – started the faith he wanted to gets the Jews onboard right?

GAB: He needed an accountant, did he?

MUSH: So he tried to introduce your day of fasting –

GAB: Yom Kippur –

MUSH: Yeah, into Islam. To ease the transition. And the Jews still weren't interested in converting so he was just like, 'Ok. Cool. *We'll* do a *month* of fasting then.' That's why Ramadan's a month long.

GAB: I don't believe that.

MUSH: Google it.

GAB: If this is true –

MUSH: It IS true.

GAB: If it is, it makes Islam sound a bit…

MUSH: Careful.

GAB: It seems a bit petty. Like a Middle Eastern dick contest.

MUSH: Ours are the biggest, then.

GAB: Yes. I suppose they are.

Beat.

MUSH: We're not meant to have sex either.

GAB: Shut up.

MUSH: Swear.

GAB: For the entire month?

MUSH: No! Just during the day. Soon as it gets to about half seven you can just eat and bang. You're not supposed to swear either, but i'm praying on that one. Insh'Allah.

GAB: I don't think couples can have sex on Yom Kippur either.

MUSH: There you go then! I'm telling you man. Judaism is just a poor man's Islam.

GAB: We came first. We're the *chosen* people.

MUSH: No, we are.

GAB: The Israelites are God's chosen people.

MUSH: No.

GAB: Yes.

MUSH: No.

GAB: Ask anyone!

MUSH: Mohammed was descended from Ishmael, who was the son of Abraham.

GAB: Abraham was most definitely a Jew, Mush. And for the record his son's name was *Isaac*.

MUSH: He had two sons. Isaac AND Ishmael. And Ishmael branched out a bit. He went to live in the desert, got married, had children. Then, a few hundred years later, the prophet is born and boom. It's Islam. So me and you are actually *related*.

GAB: That's incredibly tenuous.

MUSH: 'That's incredibly tenuous'. Admit I'm right.

GAB: In regards to what?

MUSH: We're related.

GAB: I'd have to ask my Rabbi.

MUSH: Fuck your Rabbi.

GAB: If it pleases you, then. Fine. You're right.

MUSH: Thank you. I appreciate it. *Cuz.*

GAB: It must be nice, being so sure of things.

MUSH: It's history.

GAB: I'm not talking just about that. It must be nice to have so much unrelenting faith.

MUSH: I dunno about 'nice'. It's *simple.* One god, he creates the world, he pretty much thinks we're all mint. That's it.

> *Beat.*

I guess it's nice that it's simple.

GAB: Do me a favour, Mush?

MUSH: No.

GAB: Pray for my Dad.

MUSH: Of course I will.

GAB: Can you eat yet?

> *MUSH checks his watch.*

MUSH: Yes, I can.

> *She opens the bag, bites into a falafel.*

MUSH: Good yeah? Gimme some.

> *She pops one into his mouth.*

Yep. Smashed it.

GAB slowly creeps into him until she is essentially being held by him. She props up slightly. Wriggles into his neck. He leans his chin down. They kiss.

GAB: Well this is awkward isn't it?

MUSH: Is it?

GAB: I think my cousin fancies me.

MUSH: That *is* awkward.

SCENE 4

4 September. 1.45 pm. *GAB is waiting in the hospital car park, where her dad is a patient. She dials a number on her phone. It rings out. She hangs up, she looks around. A Haribo bounces off the side of her head. She looks around. Another, another in quick succession. MUSH creeps out from behind a car and grabs her. She screams. He spins her round and kisses her neck.*

MUSH: Hello Pig.

GAB: Hello Pig.

They kiss, it's tender. Almost imperceptibly, GAB pulls away first. She crosses her arms –

MUSH: You want some sweets?

GAB: Where have you been? I've been calling you for half an hour.

MUSH: Ah – sorry. There was an accident.

GAB raises her eyebrows.

There was! I had to come down Harrow Road.

GAB: You didn't ring me.

MUSH: I was driving! Safety first, innit.

MUSH gives her a comforting squeeze on her nape. She pulls away a little.

MUSH: You ok?

GAB: Yeah!

MUSH grabs her hand to lead her out of the car park. She resists.

MUSH: Come on.

GAB: My sister's getting here at 2.

MUSH: Oh fff…is it…

He checks his watch. GAB pulls him in, gives him a little kiss.

GAB: Sorry…she's already on her way, otherwise I would definitely –

She knows I'm here.

I'm really sorry but you have to go.

MUSH: What – right now?

GAB: You can't stay here. She's on her way.

MUSH: Are you actually serious or…?

GAB: Well, yeah. I'm so super sorry, but I said I had an *hour*, that was 45 minutes ago.

MUSH: It's not my fault, though, there was traffic.

GAB: It's really crappy timing, I know, but Becky's literally 5 minutes away. Let's meet tonight or tomorrow or something, yeah? Mush?

MUSH turns around and bends over. He sighs.

Beat.

MUSH: Go on then.

Beat.

MUSH: Fuck me.

(N.B. This is in no way aggressive – It's meant in jest.)

GAB: What?

MUSH: Fuck me over. Again.

GAB: Get up!

MUSH: Don't be shy. It's your favourite thing!

GAB tries to pull him up. She's laughing but also embarrassed. He's resistant.

GAB: Mush, seriously now…

He relents.

MUSH: Look at your little screw face.

GAB: Can you imagine if Becky saw me bending you over?

MUSH: You look like – wassisname…Rumplestiltskin!

GAB: You're a bell end.

MUSH: I'm *your* bell end.

Beat.

GABBY puts her hand on MUSH's cheek.

You know i love spending time with you, don't you?

MUSH smiles.

But today i'm spending time with my family. So I need you to go. Please.

Beat.

MUSH: I should meet her.

GAB: Becky?

MUSH: Yeah.

GABBY's face breaks into a smile.

MUSH: I'm not fucking about.

GAB: You *are*.

MUSH doesn't respond.

GAB: No. Not an option.

MUSH: It's gonna have to be at some point.

Beat.

MUSH: You can't even introduce me as a friend?

GAB: That's pointless.

MUSH: It's not a lie.

GAB: Why would I invite a casual friend to meet my dying dad?

MUSH: Don't bite my head off…

GAB: Go on.

MUSH: –

GAB: Tell me then, I'm not telepathic.

MUSH: I feel like you should tell him about us. While you still can.

GAB: No, Mush.

MUSH: Why not? Doesn't he want you to be happy?

GAB: It's way more complicated than that, and you *know* it is. He's very fragile. You're making it sound/ trivial.

MUSH: Simple?

GAB: Oh come on…

MUSH: 'Hi, this is my new boyfriend.' That's it. Easy.

GAB: Ok – Then why haven't I met *your* family?

MUSH: Fine! Let's do it then. We can go right after I've met yours.

GAB: No. Becky'll laugh in my face –

Mush: –

GAB: I don't mean that in a horrible way, but she will, they both will. I'm just trying to protect all of you.

MUSH: Or you're embarrassed of me.

GAB: Can we talk about this/ later?

MUSH: No. *No*. I'm *tired* of this! We've been doing this for ages/ and –

GAB: Not *ages* –

MUSH: *(contin.)* – it's still a secret. Meeting up in *hotels* Gab. It makes it feel like we're doing something wrong, and we're not.

GAB: I understand that, but he's in palliative care.

MUSH: It's racist.

GAB: It's not racist, it's his faith. It's a dogmatic belief in what's right and wrong.

MUSH: You don't even believe in God!

GAB: Yes, but he does!

MUSH: So if he believes in God, he must / believe in treating people with respect –

GAB: It's not about GOD. Listen. Listen! God has nothing to do with it. It's a *culture*. My upbringing, even my school, you know? It's *genetics*! It's…my dad refusing to buy me a Volkswagen!

MUSH: What?!

GAB: Exactly! You don't get it because you're not a Jew.

MUSH: I get it. I'm not good enough for the 'Chosen Israelites'.

GAB: Oh, give me a break…

MUSH: You're so embarrassed of your Arab, call centre boyfriend that you can't even stand next to him in a car park.

GAB: This isn't about you. It's about my dad, and my dad IS GOING TO DIE.

MUSH: You WANT your dad to die so you don't have to tell him about me.

Beat.

GAB: How dare you. How *dare* you. Get away from me or I swear/ to God –

MUSH: What?

GAB: You think I should tell them because *you're* ready? I've only known you 5 minutes! Do you honestly think you're that important to me?

Beat.

Go away.

MUSH: No.

GAB: Go.

MUSH: No.

She aggressively pushes him. He grabs her arm as she recoils from the push. He holds it tight. She pulls, but he won't let go. He leans in, quiet. Eyeballs her.

MUSH: I could tell you some things about *My* Family. That my grandmother was blown up at an Israeli blockade. That my parents were *forced* to move here 'cos they were terrified. That my mum still has nightmares about the bombs. That she rips out big fat chunks of hair. She thinks Jews are the worst kind of scum. I could tell you that. But I don't use my parents as a fucking excuse.

MUSH throws her arm down.

You've been so badly spoilt by life that you've got to 24 years old and you're still hiding behind Daddy. Well I'm sorry to say this, but it aint gonna be long till you can't. Decide what you want and grow up.

GAB's phone buzzes. Ringing. They both look at the phone in GABBY's hand.

MUSH: Send them my love.

SCENE 5

A week later.

On stage left, MUSH plays on his Playstation. GAB sits on stage right, next to her Dad, DAVID, asleep in the hospice. She is visibly uncomfortable, her focus on the door, rather than DAVID.

GAB: **Hi –**

Ok.

I'm here, I'm waiting for you.

She looks at DAVID. She moves to stand up.

I'll wait for you in the cafe, shall I?

Hovers over the seat.

Yeah, but –

Sits.

Ok. Ok. Yep.

She hangs up.

GAB: Hi, Dad.

You ok?

A beat. She looks to the door. Reaches into her bag and pulls out The Jewish Children's Bible. She turns to a bookmarked page.

GAB: I've been meaning read to you, the nurse said it might be nice.

It's the Book of Job. Obviously it's not my choice, Rabbi Richards passed it on.

The Devil said to God 'Look what you have given Job. A good wife, many strong sons and daughters, thriving cattle and good crop. Job would not be so faithful if you took them from him. He would curse you.'

And God said, 'Job is my servant. So long as he lives, he will praise me.'

GAB glances at the door.

'The Devil stretched his hand over Job's House. First his cows fell sick and died. *Then* a great storm of fire killed his many sheep. *Then* all of Job's beautiful children perished in a great wind from the desert.'

Jesus – fucking *delightful* read.

You don't even know what I'm saying, do you? Dad?

MUSH's mother, HAIFA, appears at his bedroom door. (N.B. Even though present in MUSH's world, we do not see/hear HAIFA.)

MUSH: What?

Yeah – In a minute, I'm busy.

What?

She stands in front of the TV screen.

Can you move please?

Mum. Please.

He pauses the game and puts the remote on the floor.

53

Fine. What is it?

GAB: I know we've never really sat down and had a conversation about my love life, but – I've met someone.

MUSH: There's nothing *wrong* with me.

GAB: I really like him.

MUSH: Just… People at work pissing me off. Rowing.

GAB: And he's got me thinking about God again which is pretty impressive, isn't it?

HAIFA moves to check MUSH for wounds.

MUSH: Get off, man! I said a *row*, not a fight. With my mouth. No bruises. See? Besides. She's a girl.

GABBY: I haven't mentioned it to Mum or Becky yet…but I don't want you to think I'm taking advantage of you because you cant…air your grievances.

He's Muslim.

What do you think?

MUSH: Why do you care?

Azma? Ha! You *wish* it was Azma.

Because Azma looks like a fucking iced bun.

GAB: I thought you might tell me to speak to the Rabbi… He was adamant that it wouldn't work. Mainly talked about commitment to the Torah, God's word, head over heart. And that's all well and good, but he wasn't actually giving me a *reason*. I need a reason, Dad. I'm not going to believe it's wrong just because you say it is. I'm not thick.

Beat.

It doesn't even make sense. If God made everyone, why should he care who we end up with?

In the end he was just like

GAB holds up her hands.

MUSH: I don't – want – to – talk – about – it!

GAB: Like this, and he said – 'we belong to a lineage of people chosen by God and if we disrupt that, then whatever *remains* ceases to be Jewish'. Isn't that like breeding pedigree dogs?

MUSH: Yes. No. I don't know. Look, if we decide to get married, I'll let you know, ok? But right now, it's none of your business.

GAB: Dad.

MUSH: I don't need you to *protect* me! I'm not a kid, this isn't about protecting me. It's about owning me.

GAB: I know you can hear me because I'm really sweating here.

MUSH: Fine. Fuck it. She's a *Jew*. And I'm gonna marry her in a synagogue with a little hat so I get out of this shit hole.

Beat.

Do I look like I'm joking?

GAB: I'm not saying I'm converting.

MUSH: I'm not joking.

GAB: That's not even up for debate…there's no plan here. If my friends met him I would physically cringe…

MUSH: Because she's not like *you*! She's not *obsessed* with me. She doesn't shit herself every time I walk out the front door. You're an emotional leech.

GAB: They'd think it was some sort of joke.

MUSH: Yes. I know what happened to Teta, but not all Jews hate Muslims, Mum.

GAB: I don't think I could introduce him to Mum without getting really, really/ drunk first –

MUSH: Baba! Can you sort out your mad /wife please?

GAB: That's a disgusting thing to say.

MUSH: ENOUGH. ENOUGH about the *past*. Whatever happened to you is done, it's over. This is *England*, not Tyre. *You* brought them issues with you. YOU did.

You're mental./ You're jealous 'cos you're messed up and –

GAB: I'm talking about him like he's a weird knock-off handbag and –

MUSH snatches up the control pad. Stares at it.

MUSH: She's not. GABBY: He's not –

GAB: He's special Dad.

*Then…**David's hand moves!** He lifts it and his fingers spread, then it relaxes. GAB stands. Shocked. She looks to the door. MUSH holds the control pad in his hand, still. Slowly, cautiously, GAB moves toward the bed. She takes her father's hand.*

GAB: It's alright, ok?

I won't do anything if you don't want me to.

I'm here.

MUSH: Sorry. GAB: Sorry.

GAB picks up the book and continues to read.

GAB: **In spite of everything, Job remained faithful. Job said 'I was born naked, with nothing and so shall I die. The Lord gave and the Lord took.'**

Is that supposed to be *comforting?*

MUSH: Dont cry. Mum. Mama.

GAB: You're dad's *dying* – because the 'Lord gives and takes'. You fall in love, but you can't be together, because the 'Lord gives and takes'. Is the Lord a fucking *sadist?*

MUSH: Khallas, Mama. Come here. Sit here for a bit.

GAB: Can he hear me right now?

What would he like me to do?

Would you like me to be miserable till I die?

Does that serve you?

Is that adequate faith?

GAB's phone rings.

GAB: **Hi Mum. Come up.**

SCENE 6

Monday 15 September. *GAB's front door. MUSH approaches, he holds some flowers. Goes to knock. Thinks better of it. He puts the flowers next to the door step, squats down and arranges them. GAB opens the door and watches him. He doesn't notice her.*

GAB: What are you doing?

MUSH jumps.

MUSH: Shit!

He picks up the flowers, thrusts them towards GAB.

Beat.

MUSH: They're for you.

She looks at them, glances back through the hallway.

Take them.

GAB: I can't.

MUSH: Don't be a bitch, Gabby.

GAB: No – we can't have them in the house. It's not allowed. Honestly.

MUSH: Why?

GAB: Flowers wilt. They die.

MUSH: Oh.

GAB takes them and steps outside. She closes the door behind her.

GAB: Were you going to leave?

MUSH: I was thinking about it, yeah. I didn't know if you were alone or not, I didn't wanna make it awkward.

GABBY sits on the doorstep.

GAB: It's packed in there. My mum, auntie and uncle, some cousins, *second* cousins. Becky's in the back with my grandparents. It's been like a terrible week at Butlins.

MUSH smiles. Looks at the front door.

MUSH: I should probably get going then…

GAB: It's ok. I said I was expecting a friend, they won't come out.

MUSH sits down.

MUSH: How you doing?

GAB: Alright.

Beat.

GAB: How are you?

MUSH: Oh, I'm fine. Fine.

Pause.

Listen, I was kinda surprised that you text me. Don't get me wrong, I'm really glad you told me about your Dad. I guess I'm surprised that you want to *see* me. Especially after…uh…all that.

GAB shifts. Starts gently caressing the petals of the flowers.

GAB: I did want to apologise for that.

MUSH: It's ok Gab, you don't/ have to apologise.

GAB: No, I really did want to say/ sorry, because –

MUSH: Ok but, *I* messed up. I made myself a priority and that weren't right – I can see that now. / I was selfish –

GAB: I invited you over because I miss you.

She starts picking the petals of the flowers.

MUSH: Same.

GAB: You caught me at a really bad time, Mush.

MUSH: You/ invited me –

GAB: No no no, not *today*. I mean in general. Working at the call centre wasn't ideal. Not for me. And then Dad… I don't know. I'm not usually so highly strung. You've been so patient. And positive. So, you know. Thanks for that.

MUSH: I think you're naturally highly strung.

GAB: *(Fast.)* No I'm not. How?

MUSH: I remember very passionately debating the existence of God in the pub.

GAB: That doesn't make me –

MUSH: Gotcha.

MUSH winks. GAB smiles.

Well I may have missed the point on that one too. Maybe not *God*, I don't like that automatic assumption that it's 'God', but… Don't you think it's weird that you come into my life just as Dad leaves? Cosmic flow maybe? Karma? I don't know. I need to think about it more.

MUSH: You don't have to say that for my benefit.

GAB: I'm not. I'm not saying it for your benefit at all, but you must admit the timing is bizarre.

Beat.

I told him about you, you know – a couple of days after I last saw you. He'd pretty much stopped talking by then, but I'm sure he could hear me.

MUSH: Yeah?

GAB: He moved his hand. Like this.

She stops picking petals to repeat David's hand action. It's very precise – etched on her mind.

The nurse said it could've been any number of things, you know, dreaming, stretching, just a twitch. I feel like he was either trying to hold my hand, or he was trying to strangle me.

MUSH: No. It definitely wouldn't of been that.

GAB: It doesn't matter now, does it?

Beat.

MUSH: I told *my* parents.

GAB: When?

MUSH: About a week ago. She could tell something was up, so I just told her and she can be quite intense when I'm upset, you know? She follows me round the house and shit – it winds me up. So I just sat them down and told them. I'd met this Jewish girl, that it was getting serious. I said we'd had a big row butI still…have strong feelings for you.

GAB: I bet she thinks I'm a total bitch.

MUSH: Yeah. She cried. But she's always crying because she's a psycho. Don't worry about it.

GAB: What about your dad?

MUSH: He was a lot more chilled. He weren't horrible or nothing… He just says it like it is, my dad.

He makes a mental/mind gesture.

GAB: ?

MUSH: **The bear came to dance, he killed seven or eight people.**

Beat.

It means 'The bear came to the dance but accidentally murdered people.'

They chuckle. GAB offers him her palm, face up. Wiggles her fingers.

It means some things just don't work, even when you want them to. Cause you end up hurting people.

Pause. She lowers her hand.

It made me think about us. You and me, we don't…fit right, do we? People should *fit*. I know they say opposites attract or whatever and that might be true, but how long does that last? You're ambitious and complicated so you always wanna *question* everything. Every little thing. Don't get me wrong, I think it's fucking great. It's kind of what made me fancy you in the first place. But you've also got this religion –

GAB: I don't –

MUSH: – *way of life*, then – that I don't *fit* into. You know what I mean, don't you Gab?

GAB: I never wanted to change you.

Beat.

Why did you come here?

MUSH: Because…you asked me to. I still want to be your friend –

GAB: Do you love me?

MUSH: I don't know –

GAB: I love *you*.

MUSH: Maybe you think you do now, but –

GAB: What's wrong with now?

He goes to hold her.

No – fuck off a minute – I'm talking. What's wrong with now?

MUSH: I'm not saying I wanna get married and have kids and that, but one day I will. I want a future I can look forward to.

GAB: Fuck the future, the future doesn't exist! Now exists! I've spent too long worrying about that kind of nonsense. How's it going to work, what I think, what you think, what my dad thinks, even what God thinks, and that's not the point, is it? The point is that time is a luxury and the people you love get snatched away from you. They do!

Don't touch me – I'm trying to talk.

I *refuse,* I absolutely *refuse* to lose you as well. Not when I have a choice. Do you understand? So don't tell me you don't know and you're not sure and you're getting the willies, because it's not flipping good enough.

MUSH: Wow.

GAB: Don't talk crap then!

Beat.

You're here and I want you here. Very much. That's kind of it. It's simple, right?

GABBY picks out some petals from the flowers and dabs her wrists.

Me and Becks used to pretend to make perfume like this.

MUSH: Does it work?

GABBY offers him her wrist.

Smells like a can of Glade.

GAB: It's nice!

MUSH: Me and Farouk used to piss in the post box and wait for the postman.

They laugh. He touches her cheek.

GAB: I don't think either of us needs to change for this to work.

Beat. GABBY places the remains of the flowers next to the doorstep, stands up.

GAB: Do you want a cup of tea?

MUSH: Where?

GAB: In the kitchen.

She pushes the door open.

Come in.

MUSH: You want me to go in there?

GAB: I want you to meet my family.

Beat.

MUSH: They're going to hate me.

GAB: Maybe. Come on.

End.

WWW.OBERONBOOKS.COM

 Follow us on www.twitter.com/@oberonbooks
& www.facebook.com/OberonBooksLondon